EXPLORING SMART CITIES ACTIVITY BOOK FOR KIDS

Written and Created by
Dr. Jonathan Reichental
& Brett Hoffstadt

This book belongs to:

First Edition July 2021

Cover design by Safeer Ahmed

Copyright © 2021
Dr. Jonathan Reichental
& Brett Hoffstadt
All Rights Reserved

ISBN: 978-1-7376099-0-2

www.smartcitybook.com/kids

This book is a product of
Innovation Fountain
www.innovationfountain.com

Made with love in California, USA

Dedications

I dedicate this book to the beautiful children and adults lost at Sandy Hook Elementary School, Newtown, Connecticut on December 14, 2012. They will forever be in my thoughts.

                                              Dr. Jonathan Reichental, July 2021

I dedicate this book to the technology innovators of our world - past, present, and future - who still remember, respect, and rejoice their humanity while they embrace advanced technologies. Let us remember who (and what) is meant to serve whom. To those future innovators, may you successfully value and respect human life above all else.

                                                    Brett Hoffstadt, July 2021

Contents

Ready for an Adventure?	1
Getting the Most from this Book	2
Section 1 - History of Cities	3
Section 2 - Cities Today	21
Section 3 - Future of Cities	49
Solutions	85
Glossary	101
About the Authors	107
Acknowledgements	109
Additional Resources	111

Ready for an Adventure?

Congratulations, Explorer!

Together, we are about to embark on an incredible journey to discover a future of smarter and more **sustainable** cities.

Today, more than half of the people in the world live in cities. In the years ahead, many more people will join them. Our future belongs to cities!

A healthier and happier future in cities will require us to create new ways to get around, use clean **energy**, manage **waste**, create a better environment, ensure inclusion for all, and do much more.

Creating and adopting new ideas that improve quality of life is what smart cities are all about. It's why they are important to all of us. Including you!

Hola, I'm Carlos and I live in the city of Guadalajara, Mexico. What is a smart city? It's an **urban** community that uses new ideas and **technology** to create a better quality of life for everyone!

Through fun and interactive activities, this book will help you understand the history, the present, and the future of cities. It will also provide you with an opportunity to create ideas that can help us build smarter cities.

We live in exciting times! Building cities that provide a great future for all of us is important and meaningful work.

Perhaps the next great city leader is holding this book right now.
Okay, Explorer, it's time to launch our journey of discovery.

Let's go!

Exploring Smart Cities Activity Book for Kids

Getting the Most from this Book

This section is primarily for grown-ups to read:

This book was written as a fun learning tool to be enjoyed often. While it can be read and played from front to back in sequential order, it's designed to be picked up and opened at any section of interest.

It's also a book which is designed to grow with a child. The youngest readers will enjoy the rhymes and coloring. As they mature, they will be able to tackle the more difficult activities.

There are engaging learning exercises for a wide range of age groups. Even grown-ups have expressed their enjoyment in completing some of the activities!

In a world of smartphones, tablets, and their associated solo activities, this book encourages kids to engage with others through games and discussions to help--among many skills--the development of critical thinking and social skills.

Here are a few tips for grown-ups and teachers:

- Encourage kids to discuss the question posed by the characters in the book. Don't limit it to these questions. Explore the topics more deeply.

- When reading to a kid, use the rhymes as a storytelling book just like any other.

- Where it makes sense, talk about the meaning of the rhymes and the questions they raise. In fact, the development of the right questions to ask is even more important today.

- This book introduces lots of new words for kids. Words that are in **bold** throughout the book are described in the glossary. Show the child how this works early on so they know how to quickly grow their vocabulary.

- A website accompanies this book and can be accessed at www.smartcitybook.com/kids. It will grow over time and provide a number of additional fun learning resources for grown-ups, teachers, and kids.

Section 1
History of Cities

Namaste, I'm Bhavna and I live in the city of Bangalore in India. Let's explore the history of cities. Understanding the past can help us prepare for the future.

Konnichiwa, I'm Akio. I currently live in the city of Yokohama in Japan. In this section we'll look at why cities were created.

Before There Were Cities

A long time ago...

Once we were wanderers who moved from place to place,
searching for food and trying to stay safe.

There were no cities built yet to be found,
our impact was little more than footprints on the ground.

But things always change, we know this to be true;
we discovered ways to live that were completely new!

The first cities began to emerge
between 10,000 - 20,000 years ago.

People Used To Be Wanderers

People were **nomadic** hunters and gatherers for thousands of years before the creation of cities. Have fun coloring the picture below.

In this book, whenever you see the SHARE icon like the one on the right, it's an opportunity for you to share your work with a friend, a grown-up, or in your classroom.

People Created Settlements

We learned to be farmers and grow things to eat.

This meant settling in one place, to tend fruit, vegetables, and meat.

With plentiful food we lost one big worry;

we no longer had to pack up and move in a hurry!

Agriculture is another word for farming. It includes growing and harvesting crops and raising animals.

What Grows Above And Below Ground?

Unscramble these words to identify some of the earliest fruits and vegetables that were farmed.

Things above the ground

GERPAS _ _ _ _ _ _

BBACAEG _ _ _ _ _ _ _

OICLSTVEK _ _ _ _ _ _ _ _ _

RBEIRES _ _ _ _ _ _ _

PPSEAL _ _ _ _ _ _

LOVSIE _ _ _ _ _ _

Things below the ground

EOPTTSOA _ _ _ _ _ _ _ _

STORARC _ _ _ _ _ _ _

SIPRPNA _ _ _ _ _ _ _

RNGIGE _ _ _ _ _ _

NIOONS _ _ _ _ _ _

STUPINR _ _ _ _ _ _ _

Find the solution on page 86

All the scrambled words above can be found in this word bank

APPLES	CARROTS	LIVESTOCK	PARSNIP
BERRIES	GINGER	OLIVES	POTATOES
CABBAGE	GRAPES	ONIONS	TURNIPS

Exploring Smart Cities Activity Book for Kids

Settlements Grew To Be Cities

Cities are different from villages and towns. You're unlikely to hear farm animal sounds.

Cities have many more people and take up lots of space.

Look out the window - is that your neighbor's face?!

Oí, I'm Lucas from Goiânia, a city in Brazil. With a friend, a grown-up, or a teacher, discuss some differences between living in **urban** and **rural** areas.

What do we mean by the words **urban**, **suburban**, and **rural**?

- **Urban** areas are the dense, central areas of a city.
- **Suburban** areas are usually homes that surround an **urban** area.
- **Rural** are the countryside areas outside cities.

How To Draw A City

1. Draw a line. This is the ground.

2. Draw a series of rectangles and other shapes. These are the outside edges of buildings.

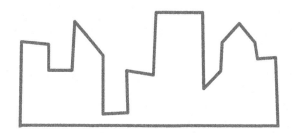

3. Draw the edges of the buildings. You'll do this by adding horizontal and vertical lines.

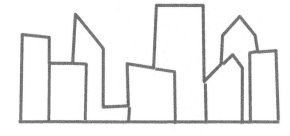

4. Draw windows and other features on the buildings.

Now you can draw a city! You have learned how to draw a city **skyline**. Experiment by trying different styles and creating old and new cities.

Cities Arrive On The Scene

If you live in a city, what is its name?
Does it have some unique claim to fame?

If you went to another city, where would it be?
Talk about the things there that you'd like to see.

Discuss the questions above with a friend, a grown-up, or a teacher.

Cities Make A Name For Themselves

Before attempting this activity, first you need to complete the activity on the next two pages.

When you finish the activity on the next two pages, take each of the 12 letters you've placed in the circles, and rearrange them here to spell a new word about cities.

You can write the letters here to help you.

__ __ __ __ __ __ __ __ __ __ __ __
1   2   3   4   5   6   7   8   9 10 11 12

Now rearrange the letters to spell a new word.

M __ __ __ __ __ __ __ __ __ __ Y

HINT: It's another word for a city. We've provided two letters to help you This word is also listed in the Glossary.

Find the solution on page 86

Exploring Smart Cities Activity Book for Kids   Page 11

Find Cities On This Map Of The World

Locate the cities by number on the map of the world. You'll find the cities listed on the opposite page.

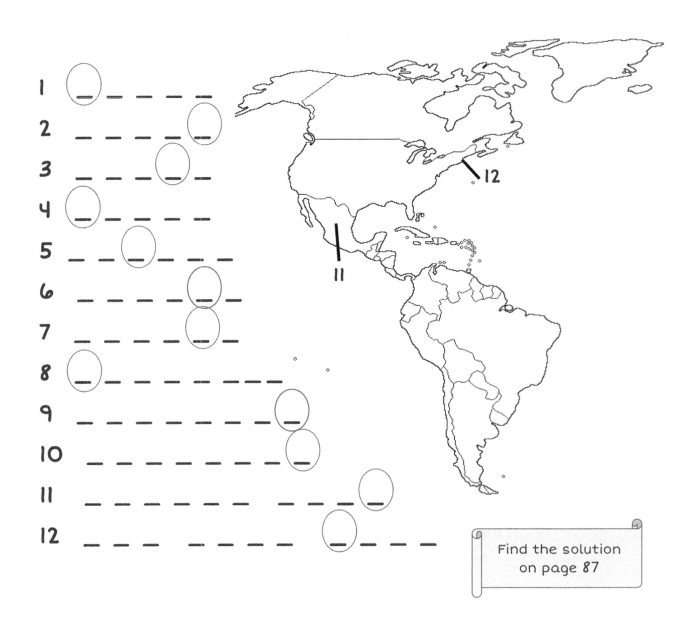

1 ◯ _ _ _ _ _
2 _ _ ◯ _ _ _
3 _ _ ◯ _ _ _
4 ◯ _ _ _ _ _
5 _ _ ◯ _ _ _
6 _ _ _ _ ◯ _
7 _ _ _ ◯ _ _
8 ◯ _ _ _ _ _ _
9 _ _ _ _ _ ◯ _
10 _ _ _ _ _ ◯ _
11 _ _ _ _ _ ◯ _ _
12 _ _ _ _ ◯ _ _ _

Find the solution on page 87

Page 12　　　　Section 1: History of Cities

The cities in this activity are all listed in this word bank

BERLIN MEXICO CITY SHANGHAI
DELHI MELBOURNE SEOUL
ISTANBUL NEW YORK CITY TEHRAN
LONDON PARIS TOKYO

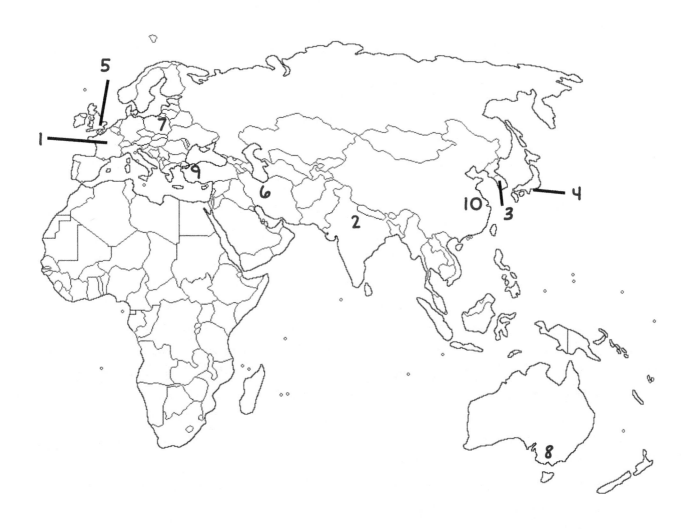

Exploring Smart Cities Activity Book for Kids   Page 13

Cities Become Popular

With cities becoming ever more popular,
people began arriving from near and far.

Many new shops opened in neighborhoods.
New arrivals brought varied services and goods.

At first there was barter, the act of swapping.
Later came money which was easier for shopping.

With the hustle and bustle each and every day,
the appeal of cities was here to stay.

Yassou, I'm Elias. I live in the city of Patras in the wonderful country of Greece. Cities became popular because there were great jobs available for all types of skills. Cities also provided a larger variety of goods and services. What other reasons do you think made cities so popular?

Cities Created Opportunities

As cities grew, so did the variety of jobs that were available. Can you find and circle all these jobs in the word search below? They may be down, across, diagonal and backwards!

ARTIST
BUTCHER
DOCTOR
MAYOR
POLICE

BARBER
CARPENTER
GLASSMAKER
MIDWIFE
POTTER

BLACKSMITH
COBBLER
GROCER
NURSE
SEAMSTRESS

Find the solution on page 87

```
N S L R Z G T P W G N R F H C I S N Z H
G Z Q J X W W W Y Z I F S N A J K I M S
K Y N F O E G K E Y V F C E R B T M O F
F Y O V C W Q X G L A F V L P R M J M C
P Y T I W H H M X H A B M I E N M G B M
R M L J F B D A T T J Z U L N L Q X R R
L O G B M I D W I F E X B D T R E W O Y
P J Y L Q I D O J Y Q B O N E E S J T X
K X B A A R D S R Y O L K E R H H I C Y
S S W N M S N B Y C L Q W P F C R W O S
L M H T I M S K C A L B V B W T H W D E
J G T B A T A M G P S C G V C U C M G A
U B R T V Q S N A G Q T D I B B X E V M
I Q B N H O Q I C K R B H Z W U W T U S
T X U A V Y N S T J E O B A P P O T W T
E Y X S R K U B K R D R C Q H M V W V R
I S O A G B C O K Y A Y C E S G P X J E
G H R W Q T E I W O D K K F R Y G N B S
E K O U U M V R C C I Y L P I Z C V N S
Y C S O N G N R E T T O P B H Y M G I K
```

Cities Created Problems

Conditions could be unhealthy in early places,
and this put a frown on too many faces.

Some of the streets were awfully smelly,
and made many people sick in the belly.

Too many crooks were engaged in crime,
this was unpleasant and lasted for some time.

An important development in cities was the introduction of **sanitation**. This meant providing cleaner water, removing of trash, and using toilets.

The Source Of City Problems

When many people started living close together in early cities, this created new and serious problems. Think about the cause and effect of each situation below and choose what you believe are the correct answers.

Why were early cities smelly? (select all that apply):

- ☐ There were few or no trash collection services
- ☐ Toilets and showers did not exist in most homes
- ☐ Horses were the main source of transport

Why were early cities dangerous? (select all that apply):

- ☐ **Police** didn't exist yet
- ☐ Dragons attacked during a full moon
- ☐ Disputes were often resolved with violence

Why were early cities unhealthy? (Select all that apply):

- ☐ People didn't wash their hands with soap and water
- ☐ Science didn't understand the cause of many illnesses
- ☐ Buildings were made from hay

Find the solution on page 88

In Time, City Life Improved

Sanitation and **medicine** reduced diseases,
by lowering infections and the number of sneezes.

After a while, improvements did succeed,
cities got cleaner, healthier, and safer indeed.

With better living being the prize,
cities continued to grow in size.

Instructions for the Board Game on the Next Page:

- ❖ This game can be played by yourself or with multiple players
- ❖ If you play alone you can time how long it takes, or you can count how many times you roll the dice
- ❖ Find one dice and a small token as your piece to move on the board
- ❖ Take turns rolling the dice
- ❖ Move your token the number of spaces on the dice
- ❖ Follow the instructions on the space you land on
- ❖ First one who passes the end box wins

Running A City Is Hard!

You are the **Mayor** of a developing city. Can you navigate all the challenges?

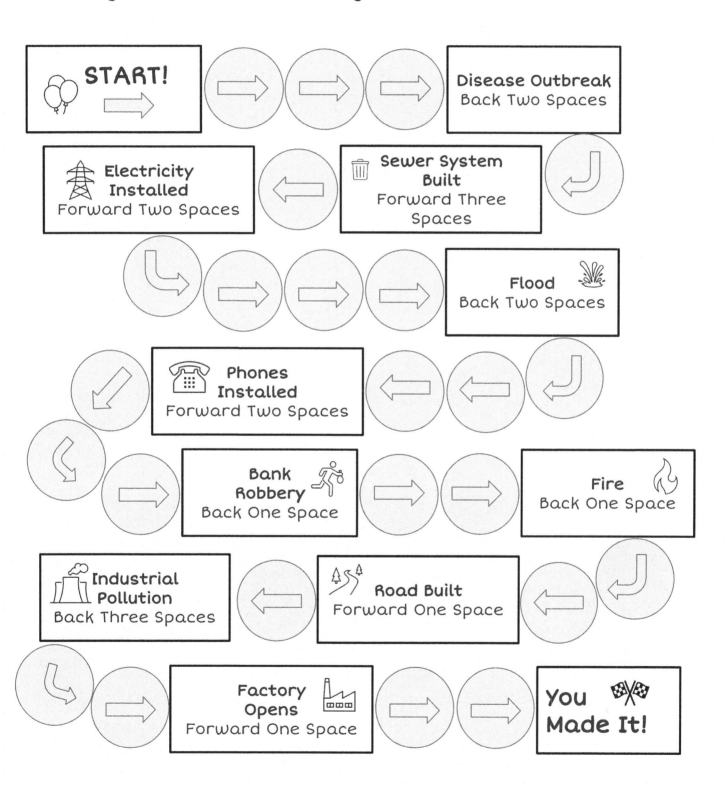

Section 2
Cities Today

> Marhaba, I'm Atif from the city of Riyadh in Saudi Arabia. Today, cities are remarkable places, but they also have problems we must solve together. We'll look at some of those in this section.

> Annyeong, I'm Duri. I live in the city of Busan in South Korea. I love my city and I want to help improve it too. Let's explore areas where cities need help.

An Age Of Megacities

Over half the world lives in cities today.
With many getting bigger, they're not going away.

With 10 million people upward and growing,
megacities are a trend with no sign of slowing.

Mega means really big. A **Megacity** is a big city with over 10 million people. Bigger cities are more complex than smaller ones and may have many more problems to solve.

Find These Megacities

Find each **megacity** on the map of the world and write the number beside the city name below.

___ Beijing   ___ Mexico City   ___ Tokyo
___ Cairo   ___ Mumbai   ___ Sao Paulo
___ Delhi   ___ New York City ___ Shanghai

Find the solution on page 89

Understanding The Built Environment

Cities have many **structures** such as schools.
They also have offices, bridges, and public pools.

What types of **structures** are on your street?
How about places like where your friends might meet?

The **built environment** (or **built world**) is the **structures** that support where people live and work.

It's important that our cities are built so that everyone can access all facilities and can move about freely. When cities are accessible and everyone is valued and included in opportunities, this is called being inclusive.

Smart cities are inclusive cities!

Make Your Own Downtown

Let's build a **downtown**. Be sure to ask for permission and to get help from a grown-up to do this activity.

1. Find empty containers and boxes around your home: cardboard boxes, tin boxes, used plastic bottles and cans, and milk cartons.

2. With blank colored paper (construction paper), white paper plus some tape, wrap the containers you have collected. Instead of paper, you can also paint the containers.

3. Now you can draw windows, doors, and other features on the containers. Write the building names on them such as bank, **post office**, and supermarket.

4. Using all your finished buildings, you can assemble different cities!

Buildings Of All Shapes And Sizes

Two-player game. Take turns connecting two dots with a line. If a line completes a box, enter your initials in the box. You then get another turn. When all boxes are complete, the player with the most completed boxes wins!

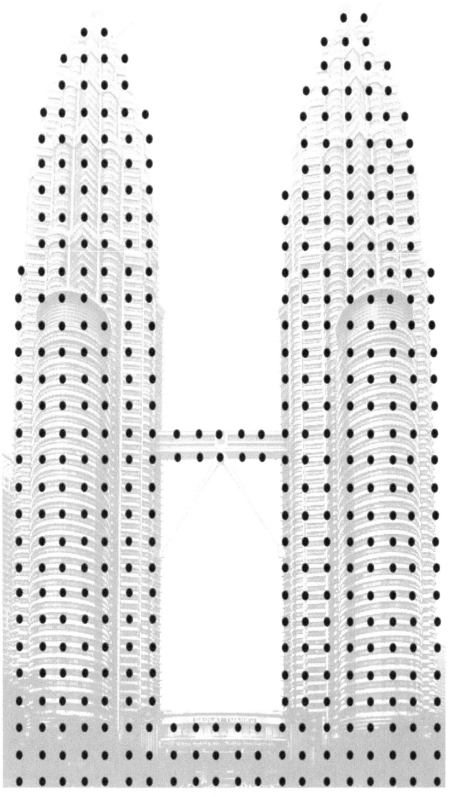

At 1,483 ft, the Petronas Towers in the city of Kuala Lumpur, Malaysia, are currently the tallest twin towers in the world!

Buildings Everywhere

Find and circle the following buildings. Look in every direction: down, across, diagonal, and backwards.

CITY HALL
GROCERY
MARKET
RESTAURANTS
TRAIN STATION

COURTHOUSE
HOSPITAL
POLICE STATION
SANITATION
UTILITY

FIRE STATION
JAIL
POST OFFICE
STORES
WAREHOUSE

```
                    J L
                    N I I Y
                  O A Y U W W
                Y J P S D N B D
              R N N S E R O T S W
            E R E S T A U R A N T S
          C G X E S U O H T R U O C S
        O H O S P I T A L L D F Q R E H
      R P N O I T A T I N A S P B K H O R
    G V G N O I T A T S N I A R T X H N X X
    G D Q H U P N O I T A T S E R I F I T W
      E P O L I C E S T A T I O N L L E X
        L Z Y E C I F F O T S O P P K P
          L D T P W O E A P E L W R H
            A B I E S U O H E R A W
              H I L P X I R Z M H
                Y P I M L I N C
                  T R T W V G
                    I M U B
                    C G
```

Find the solution on page 89

Cities Are Full Of Diverse Buildings

*Buildings are big and many are small.
Imagine if you could explore them all!*

*Some are famous and some are not.
One thing is certain though, there sure are a lot!*

Which of the cities on the opposite page would you like to visit? Find a friend and share your reasons.

Locate These Iconic Buildings

Do you know which city you can find each of these famous buildings? Write the number from the picture beside the correct city name.

___ Athens, Greece

___ Rome, Italy

___ Paris, France

___ London, England

___ New York City, USA

___ Sydney, Australia

___ Dubai, UAE

___ Kuala Lumpur, Malaysia

___ Pisa, Italy

___ Moscow, Russia

1 Eiffel Tower

2 Freedom Tower

3 Big Ben

4 Leaning Tower

5 Petronas Towers

6 Burj Al Arab

7 St. Basil's Cathedral

8 Colosseum

9 Parthenon

10 Opera House

Find the solution on page 90

Water Is Essential For Life and Cities

Water is essential for us to all exist,
from drinking to cleaning it forms a long list.

Many water pipes are really old.
They struggle to move liquids that are hot and that are cold.

Old pipes can create **waste** from leaky holes.
A smart city will fix them as one of its **goals**.

Hola. I'm Miguel. Carlos is my big brother. I hope I don't waste too much water. What ideas do you have that can help to conserve water?

The Water Journey

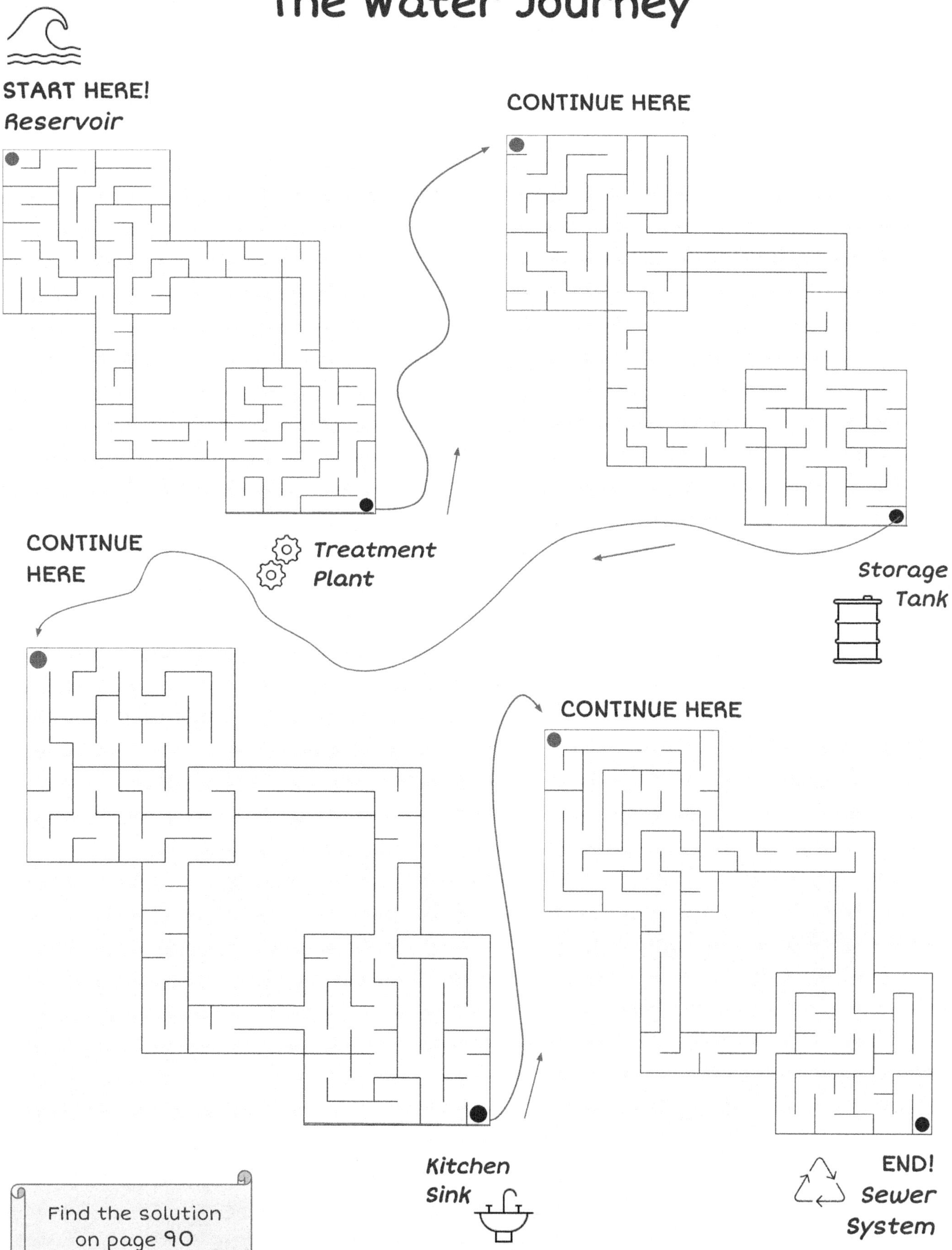

START HERE!
Reservoir

CONTINUE HERE

Treatment Plant

Storage Tank

CONTINUE HERE

CONTINUE HERE

Kitchen Sink

END! Sewer System

Find the solution on page 90

Exploring Smart Cities Activity Book for Kids Page 31

Cities Need Lots Of Energy

It's a fact that cities need plenty of power, for running the streetlights, the internet, and your shower.

In the past **fossil fuels** have made things run. We're getting smarter now using more **wind** and sun.

On the opposite page, can you find and name all the different types of **energy** sources?

As of 2020, **solar** is the cheapest form of **energy** in history! Why do you think that is?

Color This Energetic Scene

SHARE

Exploring Smart Cities Activity Book for Kids

Lots Of Ways To Get Around

People and goods must get around.
There are all types of transports that can be found.

There are trucks and trains, bikes and cars,
vans and planes... eventually rockets to the stars?

Let's not forget there's walking on the street,
it's healthy and fun to get around by your feet.

Rockets will be required to travel to cities on the Moon and Mars. Discuss whether you would travel on a rocket.

Guess The Transportation And City

Connect the dots by starting with 1 then drawing a straight line to 2. Then beginning with 2 continue to 3 and so on. When you are finished, color in picture. Can you tell what type of **transportation** is in the picture? Do you know where it might be?

Find the answer on page 99

Public Safety Keeps Us Safe

Police, fire, and paramedics too.
They are each a city **public safety** crew.

Sometimes there are fires that simply won't quit.
Call the fire service to put them out - lickety-split!

Police enforce the law on the street.
This job is called being on the beat.

Ambulances fetch a patient quick,
to help a person that may be sick.

Fighting fires, helping the sick, and solving crimes,
we rely on **public safety** through
these trying times.

For kids, **public safety** people are sometimes known as **community helpers**.

Guess The City Job Role Category

Using the clues below, figure out which word goes where in the crossword puzzle.

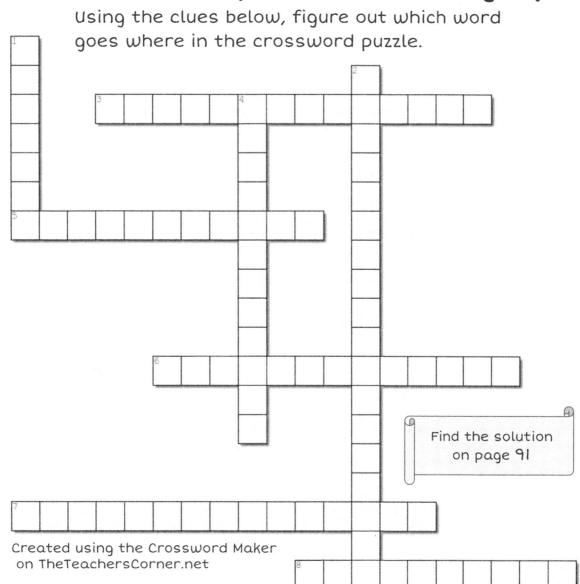

Find the solution on page 91

Across
3. Helping people move around. Roads, trains, busses, and more.
5. Using math, science, and physics to make our built world strong, safe, and reliable
6. Security for data and the internet
7. The highest city position of this type is Mayor
8. Waste collection and disposal

Down
1. Work in the courthouse is to provide this
2. Work that provides fun and joy for others
4. Community helpers like fire fighting and police

All the words can be found in this word bank

CYBER **SECURITY**   JUSTICE   SANITATION
ELECTED OFFICIAL   PARKS AND **RECREATION**   TRANSPORTATION
ENGINEERING   PUBLIC SAFETY

Healthcare And Medicine

*Cities have **hospitals** to care for the sick.
In a crisis they'll send an ambulance quick.*

*Great **healthcare** is what communities need.
It's an essential ingredient for cities to succeed.*

Healthy cities are smart cities.

These cities prioritize projects that improve the physical and mental well-being of their community members. These cities also include **preventative** health activities.

Drawing A Universal Medical Symbol

Practice your drawing skills by finishing the image of this universal medical symbol. The complete image should have symmetry on left and right.

Find the solution on page 92

Public Works Manage City Projects

Cities can't avoid some wear and tear.
Public works crews always have stuff to repair.

They must look too at things to improve,
for a city to get smarter and find its future groove.

Public works are government projects for building things like roads, schools, and bridges.

What Do You Want Fixed?

Think of four things you'd like to see fixed in your city. Then write each one on this list in order of importance. Add a reason why you think each one is important to you and your city. Use extra paper if you need more space.

1

2

3

4

Here is an example:
Repair the kids playground in the park by my house so that I can play there with my friends.

Communication Infrastructure Connects People And Things In Cities

*Messages from phones travel over air and underground. That's where data **communications** can be found.*

__Infrastructure__ is needed too for the Internet and TV. Without it all around us there'd be nothing to tune into see.

Hi, I'm Olivia from the city of Kitchener in Canada. Today, access to the Internet is as important as electricity. But many people are still not connected. To ensure that there is equal access to the Internet, smart cities focus on connecting everyone.

Unlock The Code To Reveal A City Quote

In a cryptogram, each letter of the alphabet is substituted for another character or symbol. It can be a different letter, a number, or even a unique symbol. In this cryptogram, every letter has a number assigned to it. Use the cryptogram key provided here to decode this message.

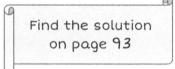
Find the solution on page 93

A	B	C	D	E	F	G	H	I	J	K	L	M	N	O	P	Q	R	S	T	U	V	W	X	Y	Z
15	21	14	20	10	19	26	25	4	5	16	22	1	3	11	6	23	13	17	24	9	12	7	8	18	2

_ _ _ _   _ _   _ _ _   _ _ _ _   _ _ _   _ _ _
7 25 15 24   4 17   24 25 10   14 4 24 18   21 9 24   24 25 10

_ _ _ _ _ _ ?
6 10 11 6 22 10

This is a wonderful quote from a play written by William Shakespeare. Who was he? William Shakespeare lived in the 17th century and was a notable English playwright, poet, and actor.

Do you agree with this quote from one of his plays?

Exploring Smart Cities Activity Book for Kids

A Cleaner, Greener World For All

To live with clean air, water, and parks too,
there are lots of things we each can do.

Look at some options and do the right thing.
Produce less **waste** and try **recycling**.

The symbol on the side of the dumpster means that only things that can be recycled such as paper, cardboard, plastic containers, and soda cans, should be placed inside it.
You can learn more about this on page 76.

A Better Way From A To B

Can you think of cleaner and less **energy-**consuming ways of traveling to each of the following places nearest to your home?

1. School _____
2. Park _____
3. Work _____
4. Doctor _____
5. Hairdresser _____
6. Countryside _____
7. Another city close to yours _____
   _____
8. Supermarket _____
9. Mall _____
10. Favorite restaurant _____

Here are some hints:
Walk, cycle, bus, train, run, subway, electric bike, and boat.

City Scavenger Hunt

Let's have some fun discovering the many different items that are part of almost every city, including your city!

As you explore your city, when you see an item from a box below, circle it or color it in. Play until you get *bingo* (a complete row, column, or diagonal of five items). You can also play with a friend by giving them the card on the opposite page. The first to get bingo, wins!

CITY BINGO

STOP sign	Ambulance	Road construction	Police station	Electric bicycle
Electric charging station	Traffic light	Closed circuit TV camera	Tennis court	Drone
Fire station	Park	FREE SPACE	Cell tower	Police car
Public pool	Hospital	Toll booth	Train	Bridge
Tunnel	Public bus	Power substation	Bicycle path	Movie theater

You can use this bingo card to play again or give to a friend to play with you.

Another variation of this game is to track items over a few days and try to find every item!

CITY BINGO

Fire hydrant	Fire truck	YIELD Sign	Passenger airplane	Police station
Bicycle path	Traffic camera	Digital billboard	Recycling container	Tesla car
Garbage can	Sports field	FREE SPACE	Fire station	City Hall
Live theater or outdoor ampitheater	Electric charging station	Cell tower	Building construction site	Hospital
Road overpass	Garbage truck	Solar panels at a business	Elementary school	Public bus

Exploring Smart Cities Activity Book for Kids

Section 3
Future of Cities

"Now that we better understand cities, let's look at the possibilities for the future."

"We need big ideas and new **technologies** to help create smarter cities."

Building A Better Future

Quality of life requires **innovation**,
to make cities great in every nation.

With lots of new ideas in the mix,
there are plenty of things a city can fix.

Kóyo, I'm Bimpe. I live in the city of Porto-Novo in Benin. I love to come up with new ideas. What ways do you think of new ideas?

Unlock The Code Part II

Here are two quotations with wisdom related to **innovation**. Both quotations use the same cryptogram key. The vowels have been provided to get you started.

Find the solution on page 93

A	B	C	D	E	F	G	H	I	J	K	L	M	N	O	P	Q	R	S	T	U	V	W	X	Y	Z
17			15					21						11						1				3	

__ __ __   __ __ __ __   __ __ __   __ __   __ __ __ __ __ __ __
4 12 15   7 15 9 4   24 17 3   4 11   6 23 15 10 21 18 4

__ __ __   __ __ __ __ __ __ __   __ __   __ __   __ __ __ __ __ __
4 12 15   14 1 4 1 23 15   21 9   4 11   18 23 15 17 4 15

__ __ .
21 4

This is a quote from Alan Kay, a famous American computer scientist.

__ __   __ __ __ __ __ __   __ __ __ __ __
21 4   17 19 24 17 3 9   9 15 15 13 9

__ __ __ __ __ __ __ __ __   __ __ __ __ __   __ __   __ __
21 13 6 11 9 9 21 7 19 15   1 16 4 21 19   21 4   21 9

__ __ __ __ .
10 11 16 15

This quote is from Nelson Mandela, an anti-apartheid activist, who became the first black President of South Africa.

Smart Cities Need Smart Ideas

Urban innovators have their hands full, trying to make cities smarter and more **sustainable**.

With bold ideas and **technologies**, cities can achieve many new possibilities.

Urban innovation means creating ideas and solutions to help to make cities run smarter.

Find The Urban Innovation Secrets

Can you find and circle all these secrets in the word search below? They might be down, across, diagonal and backwards!

COLLABORATION	CREATIVITY	DESIGN
DIVERSITY	ECONOMICS	EXPERIMENTS
HACKATHON	IDEAS	INCLUSION
INNOVATIONDISTRICT	INTEGRATION	LABS
PILOTS	PROJECTS	PROTOTYPES
STAKEHOLDERS	SUSTAINABILITY	SYSTEMS
TEAMS	TECHNOLOGY	URBANCHALLENGE

```
                W R Y S G                           L R J R Y
              K S Q E H A Z                       J S S N T K L
            M R U I B A Y D G X                 N O P Y T H O L B P
          J M D S R F K B J C O M             H K N Q S C U F Y E R B
        X T J T S P S M A E T I U           Z T C B N T E K W S L O I
      W C T A A S V S T A K E H O L D E R S T K E J J N P D T B O
      N T P H I T W H U M Z L F J I X N U J C C M O Q G X C O W A
      Z U C S N N U P R M K Z O M N L V K D I O S R B W E J T S Q
      E E Z S A E W U B K Y A A B Y Y A D W R G J P Q Z F Y Y A D
      C H E X B M H U A Y C O L L A B O R A T I O N G A L E P O T
      Z P S R I I N Y N R M T Y K J U U E S S O Z H S S I D E A S
      N W C O L R K M C D C J C A A V N W C I J D A T O A T S S F
      C X J J I E Q O H O N O U B U M W I G D D I C O X M V B K K
        T I C T P D G A V D O M Z V P M Z N N T V K L L F N C N
        J J V Y X C W L X D R I Z T O A O S O S E A I A J L P Z
          E Y G E C C L R Y G F T N E I N C I K R T P B I R M
            C I G M E E W Y C S O A S S G F T K S H H S T J
            R I V Y N X I U C A U R O I T A O I O X R U
              E T L G O E E N L K Q G S L V M T N E B
                A U E W M Y C Y D P K E E O O Y B A
                  T E C H N O L O G Y D T N F J X
                    I Z I N C A I G P W S N F T
                    V Q X P H P G G T N I I
                      I A S W N H G N T W
                        T J V N B R C N
                          Y M H I Q P
                            Z H W L
                              A D
```

Find the solution on page 94

Technology To The Rescue

Sensors, smartphones, and various computers, these are **technologies** that are defining our futures.

Technology can be good or bad, depends on where you sit.
In our smart city future let's make sure it's a benefit.

Data, which are facts, statistics, and units of information, are really useful in cities. Data can be used for better decision-making, **innovation**, and building trust. Find a friend and discuss why you think data is important in cities.

Sometimes, criminals will try to break city computers to steal things or cause other problems. **Cybersecurity** uses special tools to help prevent bad things from happening.

What Tech Goes Where?

Use the images of computer components and related items below to solve this puzzle.

All the words can be found in this word bank

CIRCUIT
CLOUD
KEYBOARD
LAPTOP
MICROPHONE
MONITOR
MOUSE
PRINTER
SECURITY
SMARTPHONE
STORAGE
TOWER
WIFI

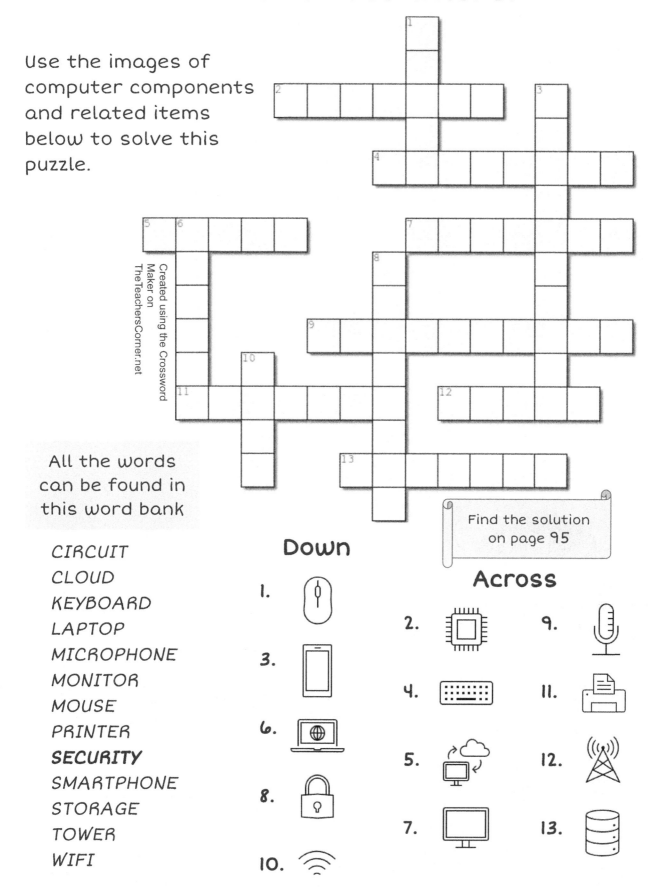

Find the solution on page 95

Exploring Smart Cities Activity Book for Kids

Connecting Our Cities With The Internet of Things

Connecting to the Internet brings more than just fun.

It can help a smart city get its services done.

For example, the **Internet of Things** or IoT, can help find out if a parking space is free.

From water leaks to **security** protection, IoT **sensors** can help with detection.

The **Internet of Things**, also known as IoT, is a Network of connected devices and people that collect and share information.

How Might That IoT Sensor Be Used?

For each IoT **sensor** device on the left, draw a line connecting it with its possible use on the right.

Find the solution on page 96

IoT Sensor

- Water flow
- Air quality
- Parking space availability
- Motion detection
- Traffic monitoring
- People Counter
- Camera
- Moisture detector
- Trash overflow

Usage

- Street lights power on when people are present
- Water sprinkler control
- City **planning** for crowd safety
- Air pollution detection
- Water pipe leak
- Location of open parking spaces
- Trash collection
- Traffic signal timing
- **Security**

Transportation Everywhere

Often it's better to walk than use a car, especially when the distance isn't that far.

For transport, it's good to have a choice of more, to work, to shop, or to just go and explore!

Hi, I'm Melina. I live in San Francisco in the United States. I love my skateboard. It's a fun way for me to get around.

Going Places!

For these different types of vehicles, write the best reason to use each one. (See the last item as an example.)

Car _____

Bicycle _____

Walking _____

Scooter _____

Truck _____

Bus _____

Train _____

Motorcycle _____

Subway _____

Helicopter   *Emergency rescue*

Bicycles Rock And Roll!

How often do you ride a bike?
It's healthy and fun, what's not to like?

Bicycles in smart cities are all the rage.
Not just for kids but for every age!

Journey To The Center Of The Wheels

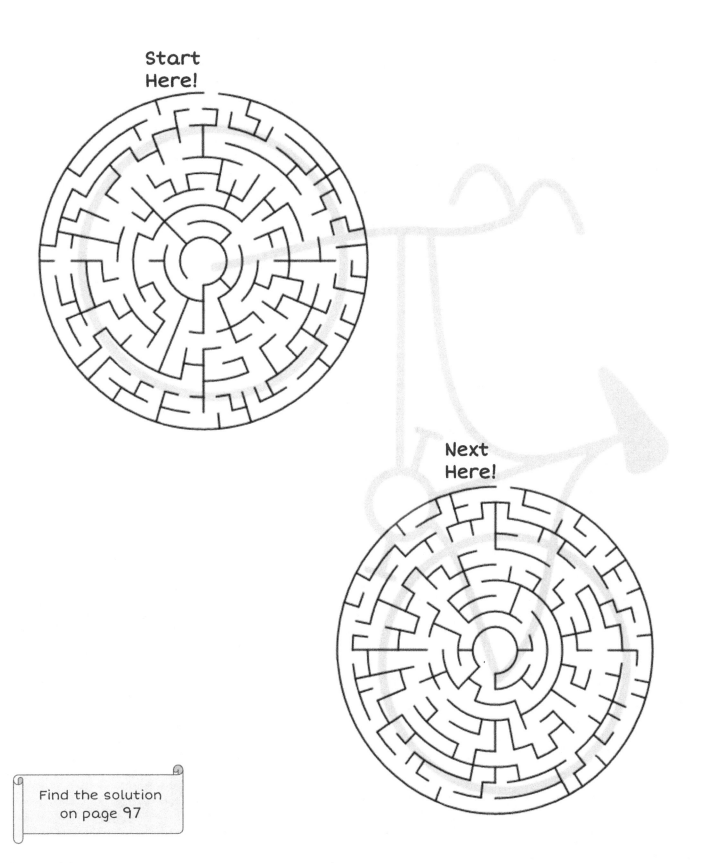

Find the solution on page 97

Exploring Smart Cities Activity Book for Kids

Whoosh! There Goes The Train

*It's great to live near a train station.
You can walk and ride to your destination.*

*Trains can be fast and some may be slow,
but they're still often a better way to go.*

Discuss with a friend, a grown-up, or a teacher, why it is sometimes better to use a train than a car?

Complete These Japanese Bullet Trains

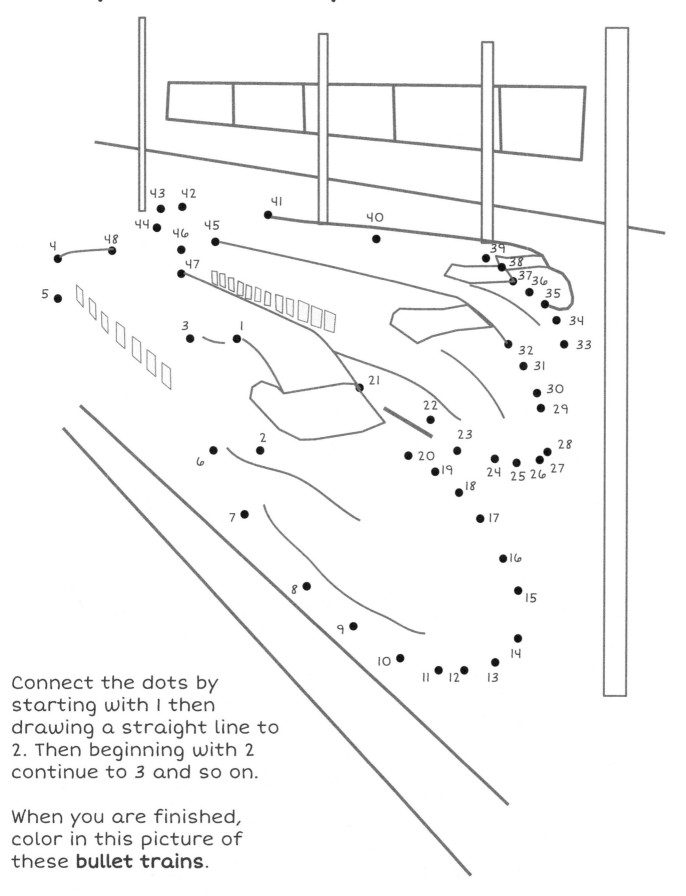

Connect the dots by starting with 1 then drawing a straight line to 2. Then beginning with 2 continue to 3 and so on.

When you are finished, color in this picture of these **bullet trains**.

Exploring Smart Cities Activity Book for Kids   Page 63

Drones In Our Cities

Drones will drive the streets and fly up high. They'll go beep-beep to avoid you and buzz through the sky.

Deliveries, inspections, and more without a crew. What do you think **drones** could do?

I'm trying to figure out what city is on the opposite page. Do you know?

Find the answer on page 99

There's a **drone** in the picture on the opposite page, but can you also find the other types of **transportation** in the picture?

Bring Color To This Exciting Scene

Exploring Smart Cities Activity Book for Kids — Page 65

Fly In A Car In The Sky

Soon it may be common for cars to fly.
You'll find yourself a passenger in the sky!

They'll take all forms of shapes and sizes.
Some will even compete in races for prizes.

How might cars that fly themselves make cities smarter? Discuss with a friend.

Draw This Amazing Flying Car

Practice drawing this picture of a **flying car** on extra paper, then create your best version in the box below.

Have fun coloring in this picture too!

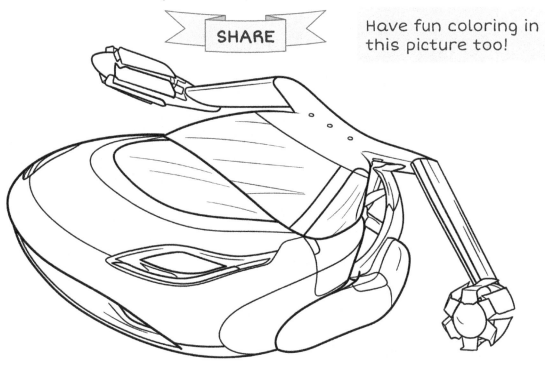

Draw your version in this box

Exploring Smart Cities Activity Book for Kids

Imagine The Future Of Transportation

Salut, I'm Hugo. I live in the great city of Marseille in the South of France. The way that we travel is changing all the time. With a friend, grown-up, or teacher, discuss your ideas about how we might get from place to place in the future.

Let's Get Creative With Art!

SHARE

Using the new skill you learned on page 9 to draw a city **skyline**, create a new city below. Next, draw new ways people will move around.

Cities Must Bring Power To The People

Burning fuels like **oil, gas,** and **coal,**
have powered cities in their historical role.

Alternative sources of **energy** from the **wind** and the sun,
are clean and abundant because of where they come from.

Certain human activities such as burning **oil** and **coal,** causes a **gas** called carbon dioxide to be released into the atmosphere. These are called carbon emissions. Scientists believe carbon emissions are contributing towards climate change. Smart cities will **reduce** these emissions.

Spot The Differences

There are eight differences between the two versions of this **oil refinery**. Circle each difference when you find them.

Find the solution on page 98

Sustainable Is Attainable In Cities

Using renewable resources as **energy**,
for our future that's a better strategy.

These non-carbon sources are a lot more clean.
With zero emissions, that's why they're called green.

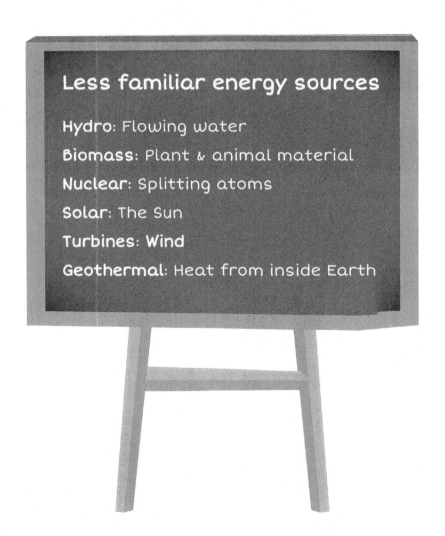

Less familiar energy sources

Hydro: Flowing water
Biomass: Plant & animal material
Nuclear: Splitting atoms
Solar: The Sun
Turbines: Wind
Geothermal: Heat from inside Earth

Where Does The Energy Fit?

Determine where each **energy** source goes in the crossword based on word length and the intersecting letters.

GAS   WAVES   SOLAR
OIL   BIOMASS   TURBINES
COAL   NUCLEAR   TIDAL
HYDRO   HYDROGEN GEOTHERMAL

Find the solution on page 98

What **energy** source do you think will be most popular in the future?

Where Does Our Waste Go?

Cities create a lot of garbage such as plastic. Smarter ways to manage this would be fantastic.

When we throw away our **waste** it doesn't disappear. Where it goes, what harm it does, is often unclear.

The Great Pacific Garbage Patch is an ocean area full of plastic that's three times the size of France and located between Hawaii and California.

Recycle The Plastic Bottle

Find the successful path to get your plastic bottle to the **recycling** center.

Find the solution on page 99

To Be Smart
Reduce, Reuse, And Recycle

Creating **waste** without a plan can no longer be excused.

Junk can be reduced, recycled, or reused!

Let's get smarter about our trash,

or else we'll continue to see a pollution backlash.

What do each of these words mean?
Reduce: Creating less **waste** in the first place.
Reuse: Using something more than once.
Recycle: Process to convert **waste** into new things.

Waste Reduction Challenge

Write down the sources of **waste** in your home. Then, for each one, put an x beside **reduce, reuse,** or **recycle,** if you think the waste can be handled in that way. Sometimes you can use more than one method!

WASTE	REDUCE	REUSE	RECYCLE
Soda cans			x

A Blueprint For Peace And Prosperity

Cities can become more **sustainable**.
Our progress proves that this is attainable.

Reducing consumption is really smart.
Our future will be brighter when we each do our part.

The 17 **Sustainable** Development **Goals**, also known as the SDGs, were created by the United Nations in 2015 as a **blueprint** to achieve a better and more **sustainable** future for all by 2030.

What Are Your Ideas?

With the help of a grown-up, find the 17 SDGs on the Internet. Pick the top three that you would like to do something about and share your ideas.

Sustainable Development **Goal:**
_____

Write down your idea for helping reach the **goal:**
_____
_____

Sustainable Development **Goal:**
_____

Write down your idea for helping reach the **goal:**
_____
_____

Sustainable Development **Goal:**
_____

Write down your idea for helping reach the **goal:**
_____
_____

Building A Better World Together

City success depends on what we do.
It may mean out with old ideas and in with some new.

We can build our cities to be smart.
There's a role for every one of us to do our part!

The city on the opposite page looks familiar to me. Can you figure out what city it is?

Find the answer on page 99

Create A Colorful Future

SHARE

Exploring Smart Cities Activity Book for Kids

Together We Can Create Smarter Cities

Big ideas and bold ones too,

we need suggestions from smart people like you!

Let's all build our cities as amazing places,

filled with joy, love, and meaningful spaces.

Remember, a Smart City is an **urban** community that uses new ideas and **technology** to improve **livability**, **workability**, and **sustainability**. Smart Cities are all about creating a better quality of life for everyone!

What Will Make Your City Smarter?

Describe the one thing that you'd like to change in your city that will make it smarter.

_____

_____

_____

Draw what you described in the box below:

Solutions

What Grows Above And Below Ground?

Things above the ground

GERPAS   G R A P E S
BBACAEG   C A B B A G E
OICLSTVEK   L I V E S T O C K
RBEIRES   B E R R I E S
PPSEAL   A P P L E S
LOVSIE   O L I V E S

Things below the ground

EOPTTSOA   P O T A T O E S
STORARC   C A R R O T S
SIPRPNA   P A R S N I P
RNGIGE   G I N G E R
NIOONS   O N I O N S
STUPINR   T U R N I P S

Cities Make a Name For Themselves

P	I	U	T	N	A	I	M	L	I	Y	C
1	2	3	4	5	6	7	8	9	10	11	12

Now rearrange the letters to spell a new word.

M U N I C I P A L I T Y

Find Cities on this Map of the World

1. P A R I S
2. D E L H I
3. S E O U L
4. T O K Y O
5. L O N D O N
6. T E H R A N
7. B E R L I N
8. M E L B O U R N E
9. I S T A N B U L
10. S H A N G H A I
11. M E X I C O C I T Y
12. N E W Y O R K C I T Y

Cities Created Opportunities

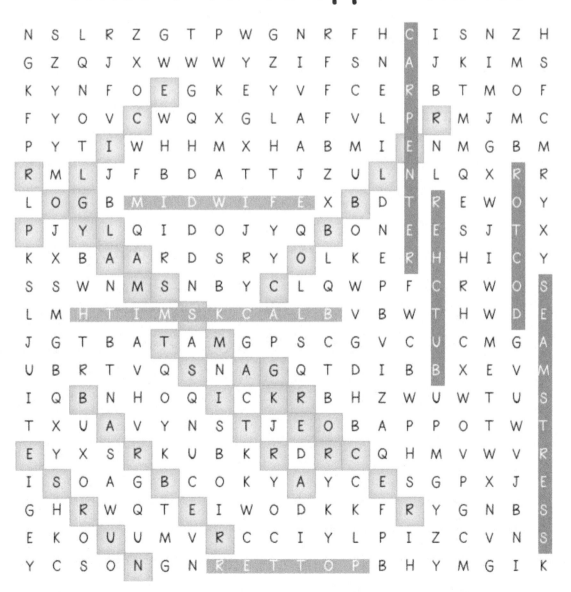

The Source of City Problems

Why were early cities smelly? (select all that apply):

- [X] There were few or no trash collection services
- [X] Toilets and showers did not exist in most homes
- [X] Horses were the main source of transport

Why were early cities dangerous? (select all that apply):

- [X] **Police** didn't exist yet
- [ ] Dragons attacked during a full moon
- [X] Disputes were often resolved with violence

Why were early cities unhealthy? (Select all that apply):

- [X] People didn't wash their hands with soap and water
- [X] Science didn't understand the cause of many illnesses
- [ ] Buildings were made from hay

Find These Megacities

- _7_ Beijing
- _4_ Cairo
- _6_ Delhi
- _1_ Mexico City
- _5_ Mumbai
- _2_ New York City
- _9_ Tokyo
- _3_ Sao Paulo
- _8_ Shanghai

Buildings Everywhere

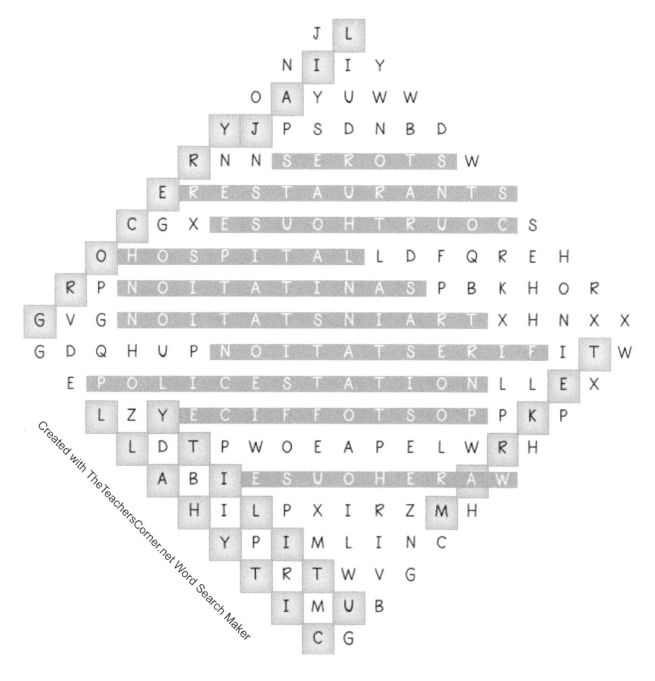

Locate These Iconic Buildings

- _9_ Athens, Greece
- _8_ Rome, Italy
- _1_ Paris, France
- _3_ London, England
- _2_ New York City, USA
- _10_ Sydney, Australia
- _6_ Dubai, UAE
- _5_ Kuala Lumpur, Malaysia
- _4_ Pisa, Italy
- _7_ Moscow, Russia

The Water Journey

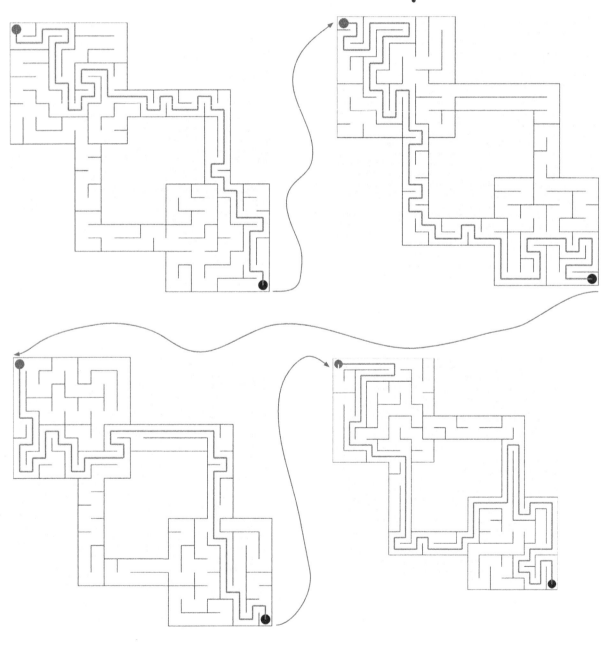

Guess the City Job Role Category

Drawing A Universal Medical Symbol

Unlock The Code To Reveal A City Quote

A	B	C	D	E	F	G	H	I	J	K	L	M	N	O	P	Q	R	S	T	U	V	W	X	Y	Z
15	21	14	20	10	19	26	25	4	5	16	22	1	3	11	6	23	13	17	24	9	12	7	8	18	2

```
W  H  A  T      I  S      T  H  E       C  I  T  Y       B  U  T      T  H  E
7 25 15 24      4 17     24 25 10      14  4 24 18      21  9 24     24 25 10

                        P  E  O  P  L  E ?
                        6 10 11  6 22 10
```

A quote from William Shakespeare

Unlock The Code Part II

A	B	C	D	E	F	G	H	I	J	K	L	M	N	O	P	Q	R	S	T	U	V	W	X	Y	Z
17	7	18	10	15	14	22	12	21	8	2	19	13	16	11	6	5	23	9	4	1	25	24	26	3	20

```
T  H  E     B  E  S  T     W  A  Y     T  O     P  R  E  D  I  C  T
4 12 15     7 15  9  4    24 17  3     4 11     6 23 15 10 21 18  4

T  H  E     F  U  T  U  R  E     I  S     T  O     C  R  E  A  T  E
4 12 15    14  1  4  1 23 15    21  9     4 11    18 23 15 17  4 15

I  T .
21 4
```

A quote from Alan Kay

```
I  T     A  L  W  A  Y  S     S  E  E  M  S
21 4    17 19 24 17  3  9     9 15 15 13  9

I  M  P  O  S  S  I  B  L  E     U  N  T  I  L     I  T     I  S
21 13 6 11  9  9 21  7 19 15     1 16  4 21 19    21  4    21  9

D  O  N  E .
10 11 16 15
```

A quote from Nelson Mandela

Find the Urban Innovation Secrets

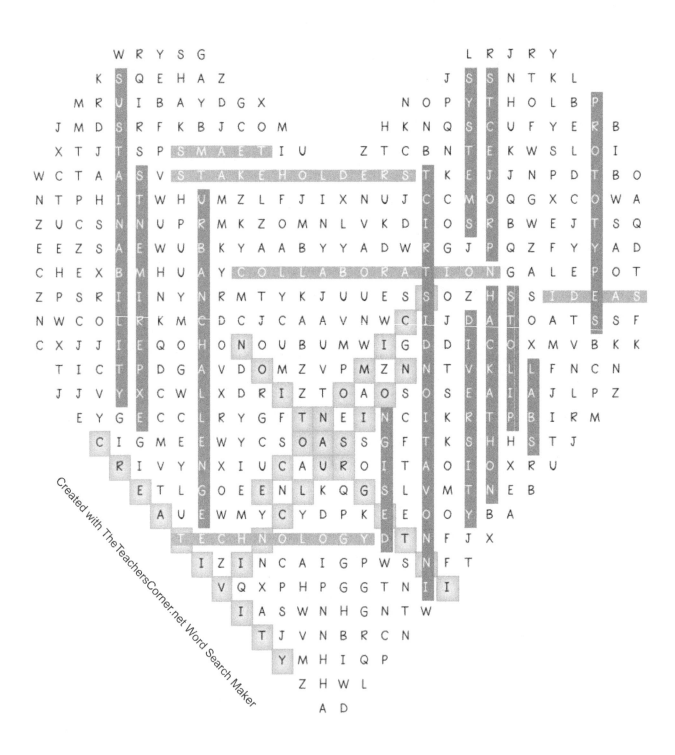

What Tech Goes Where?

How Might That IoT Sensor Be Used?

IoT Sensor	Usage
Water flow	Street lights power on when people are present
Air quality	Water sprinkler control
Parking space availability	City **planning**
Motion detection	Air pollution detection
Traffic monitoring	Water pipe leak
Counter	Location of open parking spaces
Camera	Trash collection
Trash monitor	Traffic signal timing
Moisture detector	**Security**

Matches:
- Water flow → Water pipe leak
- Air quality → Air pollution detection
- Parking space availability → Location of open parking spaces
- Motion detection → Street lights power on when people are present
- Traffic monitoring → Traffic signal timing
- Counter → City planning
- Camera → Security
- Trash monitor → Trash collection
- Moisture detector → Water sprinkler control

Journey To The Center Of The Wheels

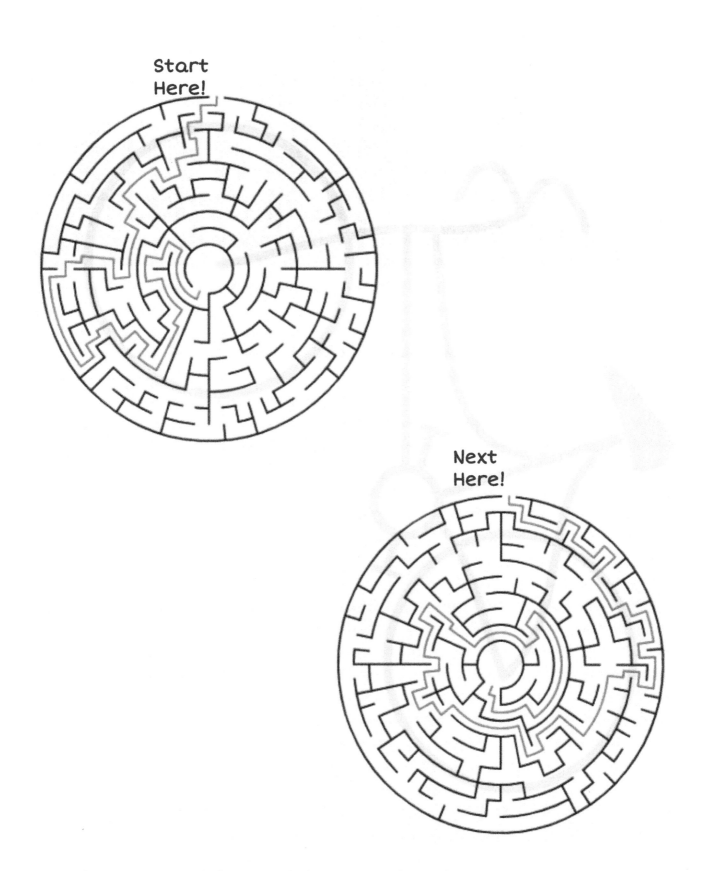

Exploring Smart Cities Activity Book for Kids   Page 97

Spot the Differences

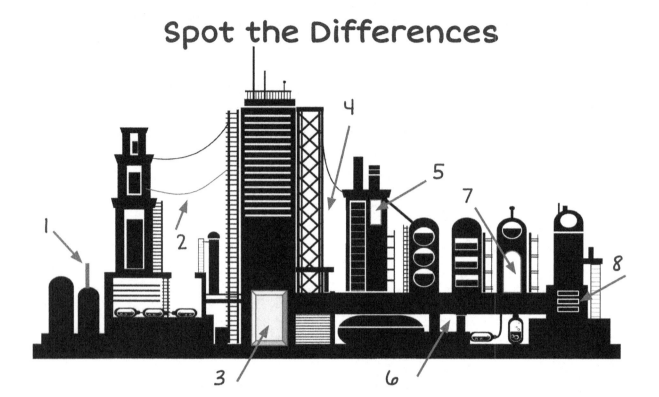

Where Does the Energy Fit?

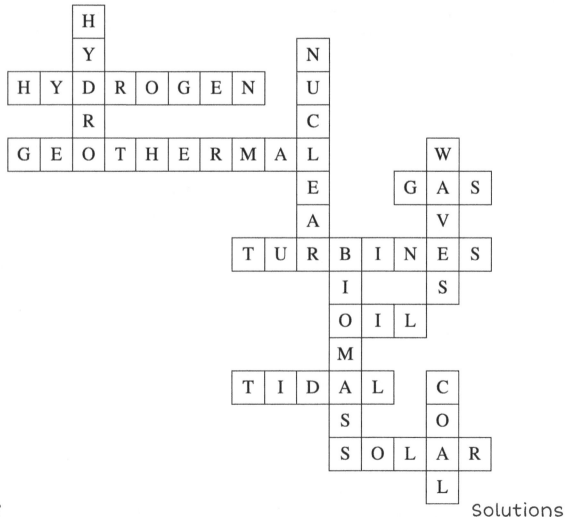

Page 98

Solutions

Recycle The Plastic Bottle

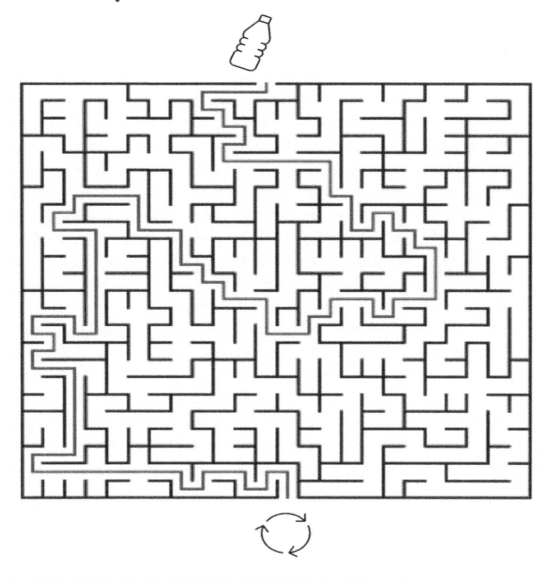

Guess What City It Is

There were scenes from three cities around the world in this book that we asked you to guess what they were. Here are the answers. They are also all **megacities**. How did you do?

Page 35: Amsterdam, The Netherlands
Page 65: Shanghai, China
Page 81: New York City, United States of America

Glossary

A

Agriculture	Growing and harvesting crops and raising animals

B

Barber	Person who cuts and styles hair
Biomass	Plant or animal material used as fuel to produce electricity or heat
Blacksmith	Person who makes things from steel and iron
Blueprint	Drawing that shows people how to build something
Built Environment	Structures that support where people live and work
Bullet Train	High-speed passenger train
Butcher	Person who carves and sells meat

C

Carpenter	Person who builds things out of wood
City hall	Building for city workers
Coal	Fuel that is the result of plants being turned into fossils
Cobbler	Person who makes and repairs shoes
Collaboration	Working together with others for a common goal
Communication	Sending messages between things or people
Community Helpers	Person who helps with the well-being of others in the community
Courthouse	Building that contains courts for holding law hearings and jury trials
Cybersecurity	Protecting computers from criminals

D

District	Section of a city
Diversity	Things or or a group of people with variety
Doctor	Person who treats sick or injured people
Downtown	Central area of a city with a lot of business activity
Drone	Unpiloted ground, water, or air vehicle

E

Economics	Subject of how goods and services are produced and consumed
Emergency	Unexpected situation that presents serious risks
Energy	Power to do work
Engineering	Applying science, problem solving, and creativity to design, build, and operate things
Experiment	Activity without a known result performed in order to learn something

F

Fire Station	Building that contains and supports fire fighters and their equipment such as fire trucks
Flying Car	Vehicle that can operate on roads as well as in the air
Fossil Fuel	Fuel that comes from the ancient remains of plants or animals. Examples are oil, gas, and coal.

G

Gas	Fossil fuel that is in gas form
Geothermal	Energy that uses temperature differences (thermal) in the ground (geo) to generate power
Glassmaker	Person who makes objects out of glass
Goal	Desired result of an effort
Grocer	Person who operates a store that sells food

H

Hackathon	Event where people collaborate to quickly create a basic solution
Healthcare	Services to prevent and treat sick people
Hospital	Building where doctors, nurses, and healthcare workers provide healthcare
Hydro	Use of water such as hydropower which is energy from the motion of water
Hydrogen	Light and abundant element of nature. The first element on the periodic table

I

Inclusion	Taking care to include people who are typically not included
Infrastructure	Basic physical items in a city such as bridges, roads, poles, and pipes
Innovation	Idea that is made into a new product or service
Integration	In solutions this is the process of uniting different things
Internet of Things (IoT)	Network of connected devices and people that collect and share information

J

Jail	Building where people who commit crimes are held as punishment

L

Lab	Place for creating experiments
Livability	The degree to which conditions produce a better quality of life

M

Mayor	Person elected to help run a city
Medicine	Practice of dealing with disease or injury
Megacity	City with at least 10 million people
Midwife	Person who assists with childbirth
Municipality	Another word for a type of city

N

Nomadic	Act of wandering and not living in any permanent place. These people are called Nomads.
Nuclear	Type of energy created using atoms
Nurse	Medical worker who takes care of the sick and injured and also assists doctors

O

Oil	Fossil fuel mainly composed of plants that have turned into liquid over a long period of time

P

Pilot	Trying an experiment first to see whether it makes sense to build something
Planning	Thinking of all the activities needed to reach a goal
Police	People responsible for enforcing laws, arresting people, and preserving peace in a community.
Police station	Building where police work when they are not out in the community
Post Office	Building where mail and packages are processed for delivery
Potter	Person who builds and sells items made of clay
Preventative	Protecting or guarding against serious harm, damage, or injury; being proactive
Prototype	Version of a solution that is tested with customers
Public Safety	Government work dedicated to the health, safety, and security of communities
Public Works	Government projects for building things like roads, schools, and bridges

R

Recreation	Activity that provides fun and relaxation from work
Recycling	Process to convert waste into new things
Reduce	Creating less waste in the first place
Refinery	Facility that processes oil so that it can be used for energy
Reuse	Using something more than once
Rural	Countryside area away from a city

S

Sanitation	Products and services for keeping people away from waste and disease in order to maintain health
Seamstress	Person who makes clothes by sewing
Security	Protecting people from harm
Sensor	Device that detects changes in the environment
Skyline	Shapes a group of city buildings make against the sky
Solar	Related to the sun such as solar energy which is energy created by sunshine
Stakeholder	Person who is interested in the result of an effort or who will be affected by it
Stores	Buildings in a city where products or services are provided
Structure	Item made by people such as buildings and bridges
Suburban	Area with houses between a city downtown and the countryside
Sustainability	Ability to meet needs today while preserving the needs of the future
Sustainable	Able to be maintained for many years
System	Group of items that work together to produce a result

T

Team	Group of people who work together for a common result
Technology	Something developed using scientific knowledge
Tidal	Related to the rise and fall of ocean water. It can be used to generate energy
Transportation	Ways that people can move from place to place
Turbines	Large blades that rotate and convert the wind into energy

U

Urban	Areas with a high number of people living close to each other such as a city
Urban Challenge	Goal given to teams to find solutions to a problem in a city

W

Warehouse	Large building where products are stored
Waste	Materials that are unwanted or unusable
Waves	Movement of surface water that can also be converted into energy
Wind (power)	Use of turbines to produce energy
Workability	Degree to which good jobs are created and available

About the Authors

Dr. Jonathan Reichental loves **technology**, but more importantly he loves **technology** that improves lives and makes people happier. He is fascinated by cities too. He recognizes that cities have lots of problems to solve and enjoys helping to create and deliver bold solutions, often using **technology**. Jonathan is also a passionate educator who teaches at several universities and creates online learning videos. He wrote the best seller, Smart Cities for Dummies. You can contact him and also learn more about his interests and work here: www.reichental.com.

Brett Hoffstadt is a lifelong learner and creator who loves combining his technical, analytical, and creative passions into projects that make a unique and meaningful impact in the world. His technical background includes aeronautical **engineering**, project **management**, and systems **engineering**. His creative energies have been expressed into outlets such as original music compositions, inventions, corporate **innovation** programs, and nonfiction books. His first book, published in 2014, was How To Be a Rocket Scientist. His book Goodnight Moon Base is scheduled to be released in November 2021.

Acknowledgements

We are so grateful for the opportunities to work on projects that matter. It's a special gift and privilege we've both been given.

In creating this book, we want to thank a number of people and organizations who helped to make it possible.

Thanks to the creators at PuzzleFast and TheTeachersCorner for their word puzzle generators.

Big appreciation to Pixabay and Microsoft for providing so many royalty and attribution-free icons, images, and clipart.

Thanks to Freepik.com and brgfx (https://www.freepik.com/brgfx) for all the character images throughout the book

We're grateful to Google for providing so many free online tools. We used many of them in producing this book.

We're thankful for the brilliant teachers who reviewed the book draft and provided essential feedback: Deborah Foehrkolb Belcourt, Robert Foster, Kelly Gary Kostakis, and Bernadette Brandsma.

(By the way, we love and appreciate all teachers.)

To anyone who gave us advice, did work, or just listened when we needed someone to listen, we thank you.

Finally, our biggest thanks is for YOU, the explorer! We thank you both for your interest in the important topic of the future of our cities and for being part of our journey.

Jonathan & Brett

Additional Resources

You can find more activities and fun at this book's website: www.smartcitybook.com/kids

For grown-ups and big kids, check out Dr. Reichental's comprehensive and fun book for building better cities, *Smart Cities for Dummies*, here:

www.smartcitybook.com

You can also find lots of videos and articles on smart cities and other topics at his website: www.reichental.com

Brett has produced many other activity books. Be sure to check them out and learn more here:

www.HowToBeaRocketScientist.com

Copyright © 2021
Dr. Jonathan Reichental
& Brett Hoffstadt
All Rights Reserved

This book is a product of
Innovation Fountain
www.innovationfountain.com

For bulk and school orders, contact us through
www.smartcitybook.com/kids

Made with love in California, USA

Notes

Notes

Made in United States
Orlando, FL
03 June 2022